100

things you should know about

BEARS

Camilla de la Bedoyere

Consultant: Barbara Taylor

First published as hardback in 2008 by Miles Kelly Publishing Ltd
Bardfield Centre, Great Bardfield, Essex, CM7 4SL

Copyright © Miles Kelly Publishing Ltd 2008

This edition published 2009

2 4 6 8 10 9 7 5 3 1

Editorial Director: Belinda Gallagher
Art Director: Jo Brewer
Senior Editor: Rosie McGuire
Editorial Assistant: Chlöe Schroeter
Volume Designer: Candice Bekir
Picture Researcher: Laura Faulder
Indexer: Gill Lee
Production Manager: Elizabeth Brunwin
Reprographics: Anthony Cambray, Stephan Davis, Ian Paulyn
Archive Manager: Jennifer Hunt
Editions Manager: Bethan Ellish

ISBN 978-1-84810-101-2

Printed in China

British Library Cataloguing-in-Publication Data
A catalogue record for this book is available from the British Library

ACKNOWLEDGEMENTS
The publishers would like to thank the following artists who have contributed to this book:

Mike Foster, Ian Jackson, Patricia Ludlow,
Andrea Morandi, Steve Roberts, Mike Saunders

Cover artwork: Ian Jackson

All other artworks are from the Miles Kelly Artwork Bank

The publishers would like to thank the following sources for the use of their photographs:

Page 8 Renee Lynn/CORBIS; 10 Michio Hoshino/Minden Pictures/FLPA; 11 Derek Middleton/FLPA;
15(t) Frank Leonhardt/dpa/Corbis; 16 L Lee Rue/FLPA; 20 JIM BRANDENBURG/Minden Pictures/FLPA;
22–23 Photolibrary Group Ltd; 25 FLIP NICKLIN/Minden Pictures/FLPA; 26 Mike Lane/FLPA;
28(t) SUMIO HARADA/Minden Pictures/FLPA; 28(b) Frans Lanting/FLPA; 29 Photolibrary Group Ltd;
30–31 CLARO CORTES IV/Reuters/Corbis; 31(t) Terry Whittaker/FLPA; 33 Michael Gore/FLPA;
35 Kevin Schafer/CORBIS; 36 Kennan Ward/CORBIS; 38 Photolibrary Group Ltd;
43 New Line/Everett/Rex Features; 44 Yva Momatiuk/John Eastcott/Minden Pictures/FLPA;
45 Steve Klaver/Star Ledger/Corbis; 46 Jim Brandenburg/Minden Pictures/FLPA;
47 Gerry Ellis/Minden Pictures/FLPA

All other photographs are from:
Corel, digitalSTOCK, digitalvision, John Foxx, PhotoAlto,
PhotoDisc, PhotoEssentials, PhotoPro, Stockbyte

Made with paper from a sustainable forest

www.mileskelly.net
info@mileskelly.net

www.factsforprojects.com

Contents

Masters of the forest

1 In the snowy lands surrounding the Arctic, bears used to be known as 'masters of the forest'. Bears are some of the largest creatures to live on land and they have few natural enemies, except humans. Once they roamed many of the planet's forests, but now these magnificent animals face an uncertain future.

▶ Brown bears eat a lot of fish and often wait at rivers and waterfalls for salmon. They catch the fish in their powerful jaws, or hook them out of the water with their huge paws, but they have to be quick!

What is a bear?

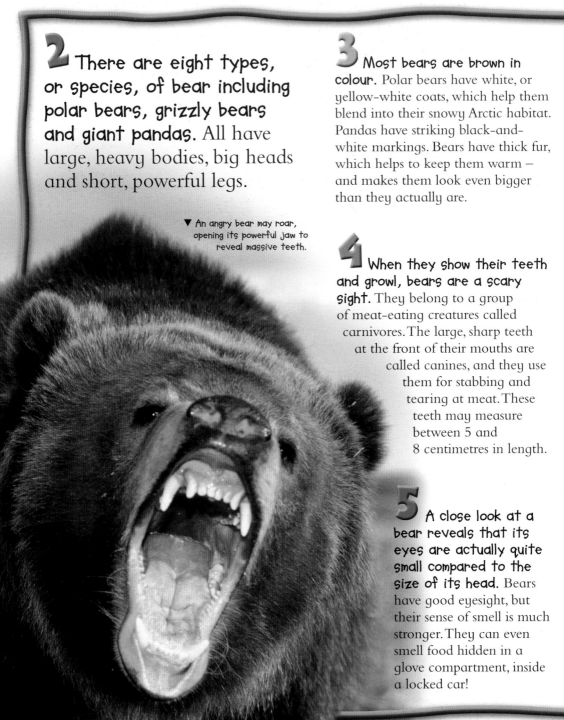

2 There are eight types, or species, of bear including polar bears, grizzly bears and giant pandas. All have large, heavy bodies, big heads and short, powerful legs.

▼ An angry bear may roar, opening its powerful jaw to reveal massive teeth.

3 Most bears are brown in colour. Polar bears have white, or yellow-white coats, which help them blend into their snowy Arctic habitat. Pandas have striking black-and-white markings. Bears have thick fur, which helps to keep them warm – and makes them look even bigger than they actually are.

4 When they show their teeth and growl, bears are a scary sight. They belong to a group of meat-eating creatures called carnivores. The large, sharp teeth at the front of their mouths are called canines, and they use them for stabbing and tearing at meat. These teeth may measure between 5 and 8 centimetres in length.

5 A close look at a bear reveals that its eyes are actually quite small compared to the size of its head. Bears have good eyesight, but their sense of smell is much stronger. They can even smell food hidden in a glove compartment, inside a locked car!

▶ A bear's paws and claws are fearsome weapons, but they are most often used for digging up food such as roots. The Malayan sun bear's long, curved claws make it an excellent climber.

6 Bears use their teeth to defend themselves in fights and to hunt other animals. They have powerful paws to swipe at their attackers, and one blow can knock another animal to the ground. Their claws are long, knife-like, and reach up to 15 centimetres in length.

▼ A bear's skeleton helps to support its weight. The large skull protects the brain and the ribcage protects the internal organs.

Pelvis

Ribcage

Spine

Shoulder

Skull

7 **Today, most bear species are rare.** They are still found in areas of the Arctic, the Americas, Europe and Asia, but once, bears lived in woodlands all over the world.

9 **They may be carnivores, but bears are more likely to settle for a snack of leaves, roots and fruits than a meal of meat.** The polar bear is the only bear that only eats meat, because there are almost no plants in the Arctic. Other bears rely on plants for the bulk of their diet, and since plants don't contain as much energy-rich fat as meat, bears have to spend lots of their time searching for food and eating.

8 **Bears can live in a variety of places, from the icy north to the hot forests of South-east Asia.** Sloth bears can even live in dry scrubland as long as ants and honey are available. Despite their size, most bears can climb trees.

▲ Bears like the sweet taste of ripe berries and feast on these in the autumn.

Many young animals eat and grow most in the spring and summer. Ask someone to measure your height now, and keep measuring it every month for a whole year (marking your height on a wall is the best way to do this, but ask an adult before you start). Do you grow in spurts through the year?

▲ Brown bears spend the winter sleeping in rocky caves lined with leaves and grass.

10 **Bears are solitary animals — they prefer to live alone.** Mothers and cubs make small families, but once they have grown, young bears head off on their own to face the world by themselves.

11 **Bears make the most of the summer and autumn months, when there is more food around, to eat and gain weight.** When winter comes, bears that live in cool or cold climates retreat to their dens and sleep through the worst weather. They need big stores of body fat to help them survive during this time as they may not eat for many months.

▶ A bear family stays close together for safety. The cubs are at risk of being hunted by other meat eaters, including other bears.

11

Bears from the past

12 *Arctodus* was the biggest bear to have ever lived. It lived around the time of the last Ice Age, becoming extinct about 11,500 years ago. Known as the giant short-faced bear, it was over 3 metres in height when standing up on its back legs. The spectacled bears that live in South America today may be related to *Arctodus*.

◄ Fearsome *Arctodus* defends its kill from Ice Age wolves.

▲ Humans called Neanderthals hunted cave bears for meat, and used their bones and teeth as ornaments.

Meet my family

Who are your relatives — and where do you come from?

Ask your parents and grandparents about the people in your family, where they came from and what they did with their lives. There may be old family photos or letters you could look at together.

15 Cave bears were hunted by early humans, and this may have contributed to them dying out. They may also have found it hard to survive in the cold climate. The ground was covered in snow and ice for much of the year, and food would have been scarce.

13 Today's bears are thought to be descended from *Ursavus*, a bear that lived 20 to 15 million years ago. Also called the dawn bear, it was the size of a small dog, and lived in Europe when the climate was hot and humid, like today's tropics. It was millions of years before more bearlike creatures evolved.

14 Giant cave bears were common in Europe during the Ice Age. Scientists have learnt about cave bears from the remains of teeth and bones they have found. They were similar to brown bears but were bigger and ate plants.

16 Atlas bears were common in North Africa, until the Romans started capturing them in the 6th century. The bears, along with elephants and lions, were killed in arenas for entertainment. In a single day 100 bears could be killed, and numbers of wild Atlas bears fell dramatically. The last Atlas bears died around 140 years ago.

Curious cousins

17 There may only be eight species of bear, but other animals exist that are similar. In fact for many years, scientists thought that sloth bears were actually sloths (which is how they got their name) and that giant pandas were a type of raccoon! Some of these lookalikes are actually related to bears, but some just share their characteristics or life-style.

▼ Their appearance and behaviour may be very different, but walruses probably share the same ancestor as bears.

18 Bears are related to a family of animals called pinnipeds. These are mammals that live in the sea and come ashore mainly to breed. Examples of pinnipeds include seals, sea lions and walruses. Despite the fact that these creatures look completely different to bears, scientists have discovered that pinnipeds and bears probably shared a common ancestor, which lived around 30 million years ago.

◀ Red pandas look similar to raccoons, with bushy, striped tails, but they have red backs and black legs and bellies. They live similar lives to giant pandas, but are not bears.

19 Like giant pandas, red (lesser) pandas live in mountainous forests of China. They spend more time in trees than giant pandas and climb to escape predators or to sunbathe. They feed mainly on the ground, eating bamboo shoots, roots, fruit and small animals.

20 Bear cats are not bears or cats! Also known as binturongs, these stocky tree-climbers live in the tropical rainforests of south and south-eastern Asia. They have shaggy black fur and long gripping tails and will eat whatever food they can find, including fruit and birds.

21 Koalas are often called 'koala bears' but they are not related to bears at all. They are marsupials, which means they give birth to undeveloped young that are then protected in a pouch as they grow. Koalas only live in eastern Australia and feed on the leaves of eucalyptus trees.

▶ Koalas are similar to bears in appearance. They climb trees and have sharp claws.

Cute cubs

22 **Female bears are called sows and they usually give birth to two or three babies called cubs.** Sows start having cubs when they are four years old, and they may only have between eight and ten cubs in their whole lives. Adult males are called boars and they have nothing to do with rearing the youngsters.

▲ Newborn cubs are tiny and helpless. They have little or no hair, so they need to stay close to their mother for warmth. These grizzly bear cubs are just 10 days old.

23 **They may have large parents, but bear cubs are very small.** A giant panda cub weighs as little as 90 grams when it is born, and is easily hidden by its mother's paw. Cubs are born with their eyes and ears closed, and their bodies are either completely naked, or covered with a fine layer of soft fur. Like all mammals, female bears feed their young on milk, which is produced by the mother's body. For the first few months, cubs feed often and soon build up their strength.

25 Sows stay with their cubs and look after them for several years until they are old enough to fend for themselves. While they are with their mothers, cubs learn lots of skills, including how to find food and how to keep their fur clean. Mothers protect their cubs from predators, such as wolves or big cats, that may attack them.

24 Female bears give birth to their cubs in dens that they have prepared. They usually make their dens by digging into the soil, often under large stones or around tree roots. They line the den with dry plants and may use the same den for several winters. Polar bear mothers have to make their dens in snow and ice.

▶ Bears are mammals, like cats, dogs and humans, and females feed their young with milk that is produced by their bodies.

Black bears

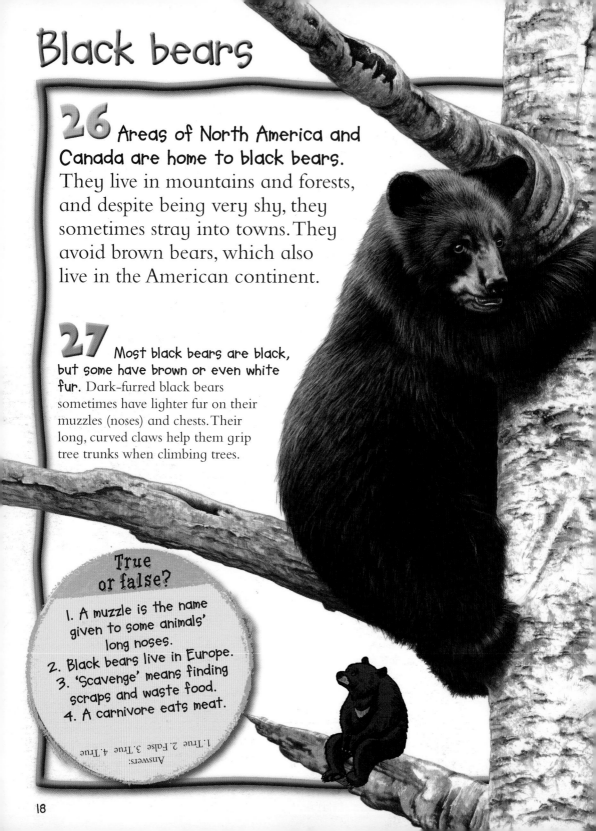

26 Areas of North America and Canada are home to black bears. They live in mountains and forests, and despite being very shy, they sometimes stray into towns. They avoid brown bears, which also live in the American continent.

27 Most black bears are black, but some have brown or even white fur. Dark-furred black bears sometimes have lighter fur on their muzzles (noses) and chests. Their long, curved claws help them grip tree trunks when climbing trees.

True or false?

1. A muzzle is the name given to some animals' long noses.
2. Black bears live in Europe.
3. 'Scavenge' means finding scraps and waste food.
4. A carnivore eats meat.

Answers:
1. True 2. False 3. True 4. True

28 These big bears need to eat plenty of food to keep their energy levels high. During the summer they mostly eat plants, but the actual food they eat depends on where they live, the time of the year and what is available. Black bears rarely hunt other animals, although they eat insects such as beetles, and love honey.

29 Black bears are regarded as the most intelligent of all bears. Those that live near humans often use their sense of smell to locate rubbish bins. They find ways to break into the bins and rifle through piles of garbage. Black bears are often found in national parks where they wander into campsites in search of food, particularly at night.

◄ Black bears avoid humans, and if they see people they are much more likely to run away or climb up a tree than attack.

30 Thousands of black bears are killed by humans every year. Only one out of every ten black bears dies naturally. The others are all killed by hunters, or after being hit by cars. Yet black bears manage to survive and are not in danger of becoming extinct.

Surviving the winter

31 Most black bears live in places where winters are very cold. This is a difficult time as food is scarce, and they survive by having a long winter sleep. This is called 'hibernating', and other bears that live in cold climates hibernate too.

I DON'T BELIEVE IT!

Some ancient people thought it was dangerous to call a bear by its name in case it angered bear spirits. They came up with different names instead, such as 'Darling Old One' and 'Owner of the Earth'.

▼ When snow and ice settle on the ground, black bears hide away. Female black bears look after their cubs in dens lined with grass and leaves.

32 During hibernation, a black bear's body systems slow down. Its body temperature drops and its heart beats much more slowly – dropping from 40 to 50 beats to just 8 beats per minute! Unlike other hibernating animals, bears often wake up to clean themselves and get comfortable.

▲ Black bear cubs stay with their mothers for two to three years. A cub learns to hunt by watching and copying everything its mother does.

33 **Pregnant females that are hibernating give birth in January or February.** Sows look after their helpless cubs in their cosy dens until the spring arrives. They then leave their dens to hunt because after a long winter hibernating they are starving. During this time, sows prefer to eat meat rather than plants, as it is a good source of protein, so they can quickly build up their strength. They catch young animals that have been born in the spring, such as deer fawns, beaver kits and moose calves.

34 **Some black bears have white fur!** The kermode, or spirit, bear has a creamy-white coat and white claws, but is otherwise the same as an American black bear. They can have black or white cubs.

35 **Black bears may spend most of the winter asleep, but they enjoy long naps in the summer too!** They are most active in the early mornings and late evenings but during the hot daytime they often sneak under vegetation (plants) to sleep in the cooler shadows.

Polar bears

36 The polar bear is the biggest type of bear, and the largest meat-eating animal on Earth. These huge beasts have to fight to survive in one of the planet's bleakest places.

37 The Arctic is a snow-and-ice-covered region around the North Pole. Temperatures are record-breaking, dropping to an incredible -70°C and, unsurprisingly, very few living things are found there. Polar bears, however, manage to cope with howling winds, freezing snow blizzards and long winters.

I DON'T BELIEVE IT!
The word 'Arctic' comes from the Greek word 'Arkitos', which means country of the Great Bear. This doesn't refer to polar bears though, but to the Great Bear constellation, or pattern of stars, in the sky.

38 Polar bears are covered in a thick layer of white fur. This helps them to stay warm because it keeps in their body heat, and even absorbs some of the Sun's warming energy. Each hair is a colourless hollow tube which appears white when it reflects light. Some bears have yellow fur, especially in the summer when they spend less time in water and their coats get dirty.

39 Polar bears also have a layer of fat called blubber beneath the skin, which traps in heat. This is where the bears store energy for the months when they may not be able to find food. The blubber may be up to 12 centimetres thick and is so effective at helping the bear stay warm that polar bears are more likely to get too hot than too cold!

40 Female polar bears spend the winter months in dens so their cubs can be born safely. A mother spends five or six months in the snug den with her cubs, while the bad winter weather rages outside. She doesn't eat or drink during all of this time, but survives on her body fat.

◀ The Arctic summer is short, so polar bears like to soak up the sunshine in between hunting trips. Young cubs stay close to their mother at all times.

Life in the cold

41 The Arctic may be a difficult place in which to survive, but the seas and oceans around it are full of life. The huge number of fish attracts seals to these areas – and they are the main part of a polar bear's diet, especially ringed seals.

▶ Polar bears have been known to wait by a seal's breathing hole for hours, even days. When the time is right, they lunge forwards to catch their prey.

42 Unlike most other bears, polar bears don't have a home range (territory) that they stay in. The Arctic ice continually melts, refreezes and moves, changing the landscape throughout the year. Polar bears have to keep on the move and search for food. Their diets are 'fast and feast', meaning they may not eat for weeks, but when they find food they eat lots of it.

43 Seals are mammals and need to breathe air. They spend much of their time under water hunting fish, but they have to come up to the surface from time to time. Seals make themselves air holes in the ice and polar bears sit patiently, waiting for an unsuspecting seal to poke its head out of the water.

◀ A single swipe from a powerful polar bear's paw is enough to kill a seal.

44 With lightning reactions, a polar bear can lunge at a seal, whacking it with a powerful paw or grasping it in its enormous jaws. It then drags the seal away from the hole before tucking in. Polar bears have to spend around half their time hunting.

Measure a bear

Polar bears are very big. They can measure over 3 metres in length. Use a measuring tape to see just how long this is. They can weigh nearly 800 kilograms – find out how many of you would weigh the same as one bear.

45 Polar bears are excellent swimmers and often take to the water to get from one iceberg to another. They can swim at speeds of 10 kilometres an hour using their paws to paddle through the crystal clear seas of the Arctic. They can dive underwater and hold their breath for up to 2 minutes.

▼ Polar bears' bodies are well suited to the water. When a polar bear dives, its thick layer of body fat keeps it warm and its nostrils close against the icy water.

Brown bears

46 The mighty brown bear is a massive, shaggy-haired beast that lives in the northern parts of the world. Long ago, brown bears were spread far and wide across the world, but now they are finding it difficult to survive in places where they come into contact with humans.

47 Brown bears are now mostly found in forests, mountains and scrubland, in remote places where few people roam. There are brown bears in Northern Europe, Siberia, Asia, Alaska, Canada and parts of the United States. Bears from different areas can look quite different from one another. They vary in colour from yellowish to almost black.

48 Kodiak bears are the largest of all brown bears and can weigh up to 800 kilograms. They stand almost twice as high as a human. Their size is due to their diet – these big animals eat lots of fish, which is packed with healthy fats and proteins. Kodiak bears live on Kodiak Island, in Alaska, North America.

◄ A brown bear can reach 3 metres in length and normally weighs between 200 and 600 kilograms. They rub up against trees to scratch their backs.

50 Brown bears may be huge animals, but they can run with speed if they need to. Their walking looks slow and lumbering, but a scared bear can change pace very quickly — and run faster than most other animals.

49 Brown bears live in northern areas where it is very cold in winter, so they usually hibernate. Some types spend up to seven months in a den, but all bears wake up occasionally. When they wake they rearrange their bedding, clean themselves and return to sleep.

▶ Male bears are called boars and may sometimes fight one another using jaws, paws and claws.

51 Grizzlies are the famous brown bears of North America. They once roamed as far south as Mexico, but now they live in western Canada and Alaska. They get their name from the white hairs that grow in their brown coats, giving them a grizzled appearance.

Gone hunting

52 Grizzlies spend hours wading in water, or standing on a river's edge watching and waiting for salmon. During the summer and autumn, salmon swim upstream to lay their eggs, and as the fish swim past, the bears pounce on them.

53 With a single blow from its large paw, a bear can easily stun a fish. Grizzlies can also catch their prey in their mouths, delivering a quick and fatal bite with their enormous teeth. Grizzlies are good swimmers, and will even dive underwater to catch salmon swimming past them.

▲ Grizzlies usually hunt and kill their prey, but they will also eat animal remains that have been abandoned by other hunters.

54 Bears eat almost anything, from berries, shoots and roots to insects, fish and small mammals. Sometimes they hunt and attack living animals, especially young elks or caribou deer. They also eat carrion – the dead remains of animals killed by other predators, or hunters, such as wolves, coyotes and other bears.

◄ A grizzly chases a salmon through the water. Salmon are highly nutritious, so brown bears that hunt them often grow bigger than other brown bears.

▼ Grizzlies stand and wait for salmon to leap out of the water. Like other brown bears, they have distinctive humps on their shoulders.

56 Grizzlies inspired the first teddy bear, which appeared around 100 years ago. Teddies were named after an American president called Teddy Roosevelt, who refused to shoot a grizzly on a hunting trip. The story was in a newspaper and a toyshop owner decided to make a stuffed bear – and called it a teddy.

55 Grizzlies may travel long distances in search of food, but they usually return to their territory. Bears are sometimes trapped and moved to other areas by scientists and wildlife managers to keep them away from humans, but a few have been able to find their way home – up to 200 kilometres away. No one knows how they do this, but their great sense of smell may help.

My Home

Do you know where you live? Ask a grown up to help you find your street on a map of your area, and then find your school. Can you trace the route home from your school, following the roads? Then use a big atlas and find your country on a map of the world.

Moon bears

▲ Moon bears often eat farmers' crops such as maize (sweetcorn). They visit the fields and tear off the maize cobs using their long teeth called canines. This is why they are often trapped or hunted.

58 Moon bears spend a lot of time in trees, sleeping or searching for nuts, leaves and fruit. They live in forested areas and are most active at night. Very little is known about how these animals behave in the wild.

59 These bears rely on their sense of smell more than sight or sound. They rub against trees, leaving a strong scent to warn other bears to stay out of their territory. Moon bears can be very aggressive if they encounter humans – they are more likely than an American black bear to kill a person, despite being smaller.

57 Moon bears are black bears of Asia and they have white or cream patches of fur on their chests. These patches of fur are often shaped like crescent moons – which is how they get their name. They are also known as Asiatic black bears.

▲ Some moon bears are kept in cramped cages so people can remove a fluid called bile that their bodies naturally create. Bile is an ingredient in some medicines. Many organizations are trying to bring this cruel practice to an end.

60 **The moon bear can stand, and even walk, on its back feet.** This skill led to many of these creatures being taken from the wild when they were still cubs. They were brought to circuses, where they were trained to 'dance' for the crowds.

61 **Moon bears are threatened with extinction because their forests have been taken over by farmers.** They are regarded as pests in many places, and many of them have been killed. In China, these bears are captured so their body parts can be used in traditional medicines.

◀ Moon bears weigh between 100 and 200 kilograms and measure up to 2 metres in length. Moon bears in captivity are able to stand up and beg for food.

Sloth bears

62 **Sloth bears live in South-east Asia.** They can survive in a variety of places, from forests to grasslands if they can find ants, termites and fruit to eat. A sloth bear's sense of smell is so good it can even sniff out ants in the soil beneath its feet.

▼ The claws of a sloth bear can measure 8 centimetres in length and are great for digging away at a giant termite mound.

63 **When a sloth bear finds an insect nest it rips it open with its claws.** They may tear the bark off a tree or dig into the ground. Once the nest is open the bear sucks up the insects. The sucking noise it makes can be heard up to 100 metres away!

◀ Sloth bears can give birth at any time of year, and the young are carried on the mother's back.

64 Sloth bear cubs can be born at any time of year, and there are normally one or two cubs in a litter. The mother protects the youngsters in her den until they are about three months old. When the cubs emerge, their mother carries them on her back until they are about nine months old.

▼ Using sloth bears as dancing bears is illegal, but it is thought that many cubs continue to be captured for this purpose. Ropes are forced through their noses and their teeth are removed. Wildlife organizations are campaigning to end this cruel practise.

65 Like other bear species, sloth bears are solitary animals, but they will sometimes gather together to share a big feast. A bees' nest full of honey or a large termite mound may attract two or more bears, but after the meal, they wander off on their own again.

66 When bears stand on their hind legs they get a better view of what's going on around them. Many bears do this, not just sloth bears. Standing on their hind legs helps them to sniff scents in the air, or to look larger and more dangerous when they are feeling threatened.

Spectacled bears

67 The spectacled bear has pale fur around its eyes, so it looks as if it's wearing spectacles! It faces extinction and may not survive this century.

68 Spectacled bears are relatively small, with dense black or dark brown coats. They spend much of their time in trees, where they sleep in nests built from branches. They are most active at night and are very shy, so not much is known about them.

69 Spectacled bears are skilled climbers. They use their long, sharp claws to grip onto tree bark as they clamber up a tree, and they sometimes make nests among the branches. They can also swim, but they don't eat fish. These bears travel around the forest on four legs, but mother bears can hold their cubs in their forelimbs, and walk upright on their back legs.

◄ Scientists can recognize individual spectacled bears from the markings on their faces — every bear has a different pattern of pale fur.

70 Farmers sometimes blame these bears for eating their animals, but this is unfair. Spectacled bears eat fruit, palms and bromeliads, which are plants that have stiff, spiny leaves. They can even eat cactus plants! They do occasionally eat small mammals, such as rodents, and insects.

▼ Spectacled bears are the only bears that live in South America. In mountainous regions such as Peru, they search for plants and small animals to eat. The males are about twice the size of the females.

71 Spectacled bears don't hibernate, because they live in warm places where this isn't necessary. Mother bears still build dens for their cubs, often in tree roots or under rocks. They make unusual noises to communicate with their cubs, including screeching and soft purring sounds.

Sun bears

▲ Sun bears are also called Malay bears, dog bears and honey bears. They have very short fur and yellow patches on their chests.

72 The sun bear of South-east Asia may be the smallest of all bears, but it has the longest tongue – reaching up to 25 centimetres in length! A long tongue is very useful for reaching inside small cracks in trees and licking up tasty grubs and bugs.

73 Apart from insects, sun bears like to eat birds, lizards, fruit, honey and rodents. Their jaws are so strong they can even crack open tough coconuts to get to the edible part inside. One of their favourite foods is honey, and sun bears use their very long, curved claws to rip open hives.

75 **Sun bears are the smallest bears.** They are nocturnal (active at night) and shy, so no one knows how many exist. They may be the most endangered bears. In Thailand, baby sun bears are popular pets – but once they grow up they are too dangerous, and are chained up or killed.

74 **In the language of Malaysia, where some sun bears live, their name means 'he who likes to sit high'.** It's a perfect name for these tree-loving beasts. A sun bear uses its strong muscles, the bare skin on the soles of its feet, and its long claws when clambering up trees, and these animals can spend many hours settled in the branches of a tree eating, sleeping and sunbathing.

76 **Tigers and leopards hunt sun bears, but sometimes the bears wriggle free from these big cats' clutches.** They have very loose, baggy skin on the backs of their necks, so if a predator attacks they can twist round and bite them!

▶ A sun bear will tear open a bees' nest with its claws before using its long tongue to reach the sweet honey. Its tongue can stretch 25 centimetres to lick food out of cracks.

37

Giant pandas

77 With its distinctive white face and black eye patches there are few animals that are as easy to recognize as the giant panda. These large bears have been brought to the brink of extinction, partly by human actions.

▼ Giant pandas only live in the cool bamboo woodlands and forests in China, South Asia. These areas are often covered in snow.

78 Pandas spend a lot of time on the ground, but they climb trees to rest or sleep. Youngsters first start climbing when they are just six months old and use their claws to help them grip onto the trees. Pandas like to rest in forked branches, and watch the world beneath them. They often come down from trees head first!

79 Pandas rarely eat meat, and spend around 16 hours a day chewing bamboo. This is a tough grass-like plant that grows very tall. Pandas also eat honey, eggs, fish, and occasionally mice.

▶ When they feed, giant pandas sit with their legs outstretched in front of them.

80 Pandas have a special bone on their wrists, which grows rather like a thumb. This bone enables pandas to grab hold of clumps of bamboo in their paws, making it easier for them to collect and eat their food. Pandas have to drink fresh water regularly, so they visit streams or rivers almost every day.

▶ Pandas' forepaws are bigger than their hind paws. The forepaw has a special pad of tough skin over an extra bone, which it uses like a thumb to help it grip bamboo.

81 Pandas are not ready to mate until they are about five years old. During the mating season males sometimes fight. Females usually give birth to one or two tiny cubs that are entirely helpless. Usually, a mother only feeds the first cub that is born and leaves the other one to die.

Under threat

82 **It has been discovered that only about 1600 pandas live in the wild.** This means that despite the efforts of Chinese wildlife workers, this species of bear may become extinct everywhere except zoos in the near future.

83 **Pandas were only discovered by the western world in 1869 — but once people heard about them, they wanted to see pandas for themselves.** The bears were captured, dead or alive, and brought to zoos or museums. We are still learning about pandas and only recently found out that males do headstands by trees to spray their urine high up to mark their territory!

Panda faces

You will need:
paper plate scissors
thick black paper glue string

1. With an adult's help cut a paper plate in half.
2. Cut out eye patches, ears and a nose from the black paper and glue them on to the plate.
3. Attach string to the back if you want to hang your panda face on the wall.

84 People have taken over pandas' habitats, forcing them into smaller, more remote mountainous areas. This means that less food is available to them. They are also slow breeders – females only produce about five to eight cubs in a lifetime, and these are vulnerable to attack by predators such as leopards, martens (weasel-like creatures) and Asian wild dogs.

85 Giant pandas spend up to 16 hours a day chomping and chewing on bamboo, and they often eat during the night too. They have to spend lots of time eating because their guts lack the bacteria that help other plant eaters, such as cows, get goodness from their food. From time to time, all the bamboo in one forest may flower and then die. The pandas in the area then face starvation.

◄ Every day, pandas eat between 10 and 20 kilograms of bamboo. They have the digestive systems of meat eaters, so they need to eat huge quantities of plant matter to get enough goodness to survive.

Myths and legends

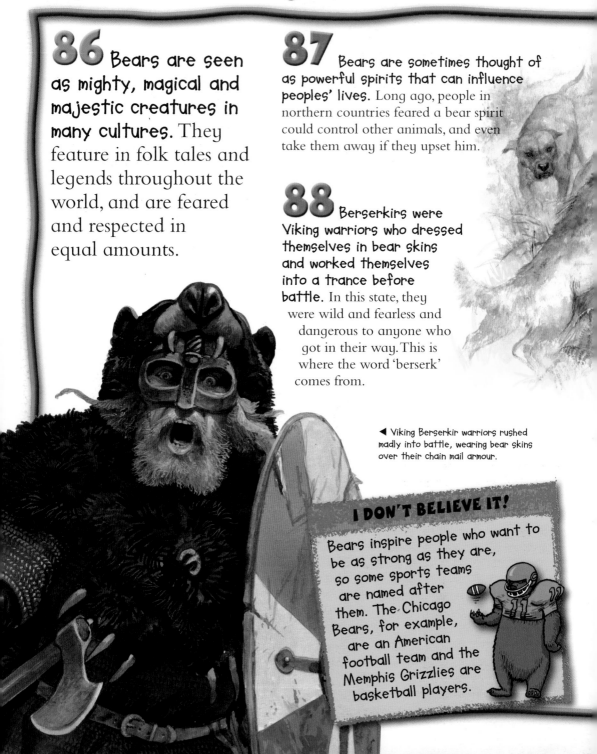

86 Bears are seen as mighty, magical and majestic creatures in many cultures. They feature in folk tales and legends throughout the world, and are feared and respected in equal amounts.

87 Bears are sometimes thought of as powerful spirits that can influence peoples' lives. Long ago, people in northern countries feared a bear spirit could control other animals, and even take them away if they upset him.

88 Berserkirs were Viking warriors who dressed themselves in bear skins and worked themselves into a trance before battle. In this state, they were wild and fearless and dangerous to anyone who got in their way. This is where the word 'berserk' comes from.

◄ Viking Berserkir warriors rushed madly into battle, wearing bear skins over their chain mail armour.

I DON'T BELIEVE IT!

Bears inspire people who want to be as strong as they are, so some sports teams are named after them. The Chicago Bears, for example, are an American football team and the Memphis Grizzlies are basketball players.

89 The Samoyed and Lapps are tribes of people who live close to the North Pole. Like other people who share their habitat with bears, they used to believe that, with the use of magic, humans could turn themselves into bears. Brave warriors were often thought to have taken on the spirits of bears as they fought.

◀ A Danish legend tells of a bear that was the king's ancestor. The bear was killed by dogs, but survives in folk tales.

90 A Danish story describes how a bear and a beautiful woman fell in love. The bear cared for her by stealing food from farms, until one day, farmers used dogs and spears to kill him. The woman later gave birth to a boy that looked normal, but was as strong and brave as a bear, who became the ancestor of the kings of Denmark.

▶ A giant armoured bear, called Iorek, features in the 2008 movie *The Golden Compass*, which is based on the book *Northern Lights*, by Philip Pullman.

Bear behaviour

91 **Most bears are shy creatures and prefer to avoid coming into contact with humans.** Mother bears, however, will attack any person or animal that comes too close to her cubs.

▶ When bears live near humans, they lose their fear of them and may even start to scavenge rubbish and other food.

CAUTION

ACTIVE BEARS IN AREA

PLEASE USE CAUTION WHILE WALKING:

- CARRY A BELL
- MAKE NOISE
- BE ALERT

92 **Angry bears give warning signs that they may attack.** These include making huffing noises, beating the ground with their paws or even making short charges. They may start growling, and their ears lie flat to their heads. Some bears do attack humans for food, but this is extremely rare – and they don't give any warning signs first. Running away from a bear just encourages them to start chasing.

93 **Many grizzlies have learnt that they will find a free lunch wherever there are people.** If grizzlies overcome their fear of humans they can become very dangerous. Once they have found a place where they can get food, they will return to it again and again.

◀ Being 'bear aware' can be a life-saver in some parts of the world. Bears are most dangerous when startled, so making plenty of noise when you're hiking in bear territory is one way of preventing an attack.

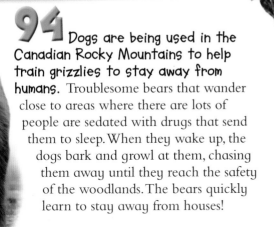

94 Dogs are being used in the Canadian Rocky Mountains to help train grizzlies to stay away from humans. Troublesome bears that wander close to areas where there are lots of people are sedated with drugs that send them to sleep. When they wake up, the dogs bark and growl at them, chasing them away until they reach the safety of the woodlands. The bears quickly learn to stay away from houses!

95 American black bears are often feared by campers, but they rarely attack people. In fact bears have much more reason to fear humans than we have to fear them. Around 30 to 40 people have been killed by black bears in the United States in the last 100 years, but 30,000 of these beautiful creatures are killed by humans every year.

Bear scare!

The advice if you see a bear up close is to slowly back away, watching it all the time. If the bear follows you, stand and wave your arms around while shouting loudly. The idea is to frighten the bear away, so you have to look as mean and angry as you can! Practise your angry face and shouting – you'll probably find it quite easy!

▶ A bear that was trapped near a town and examined by scientists as part of a study is chased away by a specially trained dog. This will keep it from returning to the area.

Harm and help

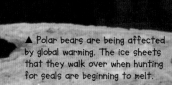

▲ Polar bears are being affected by global warming. The ice sheets that they walk over when hunting for seals are beginning to melt.

96 Bears are being forced to live in smaller and smaller areas. Of the eight types of bear, all are threatened with extinction, except brown bears and American black bears.

97 Bears are killed when people believe them to be a danger, or when they eat crops. They are also taken from the wild to be sold as pets, or to be used in traditional medicine. Wildlife organizations are involved in fighting against illegal trade in bear parts.

98 Most bears are suffering because their habitats (where they live) are being taken away from them. People have turned forests and woodlands into farms, mines, towns and cities. Even polar bears are in decline, because their habitat is affected by global warming. Loss of habitat is the greatest threat to bear survival.

QUIZ

1. What is the name of the only South American bear?
2. What is the other name for an Asiatic black bear?
3. Where would you find giant pandas?
4. Where do polar bears live, the South Pole or the North Pole?

Answers:
1. Spectacled bear 2. Moon bear 3. China 4. North Pole

▶ A tiny panda cub is measured at the China conservation and research centre for the giant panda.

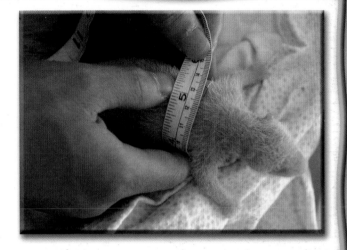

99 There are about 50 panda reserves in China, where most of the nation's giant pandas are protected. Despite this, many are still killed or captured by poachers every year. Groups of pandas are also split up, living in small areas of forest, separated from one another. This makes it difficult for pandas to meet up and breed successfully.

▼ Spectacled bears are categorized as 'vulnerable'. This means the species is already under threat and help is urgently needed over the coming years.

100 As humans take over more and more of the natural world for their own use, animals and plants are being wiped off the planet. People today face a tough challenge – will they work hard to save bears, or push them further towards extinction?

Index